55573

Vic.

W9-BUN-731

Friction

A FOLLETT BEGINNING SCIENCE BOOK

SCIENCE EDITOR:

EDWARD VICTOR, ED. D.
Professor of Science Education,
Northwestern University

EDUCATIONAL CONSULTANT:

JEANNE S. BROUILLETTE
Curriculum Coordinator, Evanston Elementary Schools

This book has been tested with children in primary classes.

Edward Victor

FRICTION

illustrated by Mel Hunter

Follett Publishing Company **Chicago** **New York**

Library of Congress Catalog Card Number: 61-10057

THIRD PRINTING

TLA 3205

Did you ever push a large box across
the room?

If you did, then you know that sometimes
the box moved smoothly. Other times the box
stuck or bumped as it moved along.

What made this happen?

Did you ever wonder why it is harder
to pull a wagon over a bumpy road than over
a smooth sidewalk?

If you live where it snows, you know how
easy it is to pull a sled in the snow. But
it is not so easy to pull the sled on the bare
ground.

This is because of friction.

Friction is what we get when two things rub together.

Friction makes it hard to move one thing across another thing.

When two pieces of rough wood are rubbed together, we can feel friction.

We feel the pieces of wood drag and catch and stick.

This happens because the pieces of wood are full of bumps and hollows.

When the pieces of rough wood are rubbed together, the bumps and hollows catch and stick.

There are bumps and hollows even when the wood is smooth. They are much smaller now, but you can still see them under a magnifying glass.

There is more friction between two rough things than between two smooth things. This is because rough things have more bumps and hollows.

Would you like to find this out for yourself?

Get a piece of sandpaper, a piece of rough wood, and a mirror. Rub some cotton over each one of these things.

See how bits of cotton stick to the rough sandpaper and wood. But the cotton moves easily over the smooth mirror.

Get two long, wide pieces of wood. One piece of wood should be rough. The other should be smooth.

Then tie string around a big book so you can pull it.

Now pull the book across the rough piece of wood. Feel how friction makes the book drag and bump.

Pull the book across the smooth piece of wood. Feel how much more easily it moves. This is because there is less friction with smooth wood than with rough wood.

When we use heavy things, we get more
friction than when we use light things.
Let us do another experiment to show this.

First tie string around two big books
of the same size. Then pull the books
across the rough piece of wood.

See how much harder it is to pull two
books than one book across the rough piece
of wood.

Heavy things press harder against the
bumps and hollows than light things.

Now pull the two books across the smooth piece of wood. See how much harder it is to pull two books than one book across the smooth piece of wood.

But it is still easier to pull two books across the smooth piece of wood than across the rough piece.

There is much friction between a heavy thing and a rough thing. There is less friction between a heavy thing and a smooth thing.

What can we do to get less friction?

One way is to make things smoother.
This gives us less bumps and hollows.

Here is something you can do to show
that we get less friction when things are
smooth.

Rub your finger across a piece of
rough wood. Now make the wood smooth
with sandpaper.

Your finger will move more easily
across the smooth wood.

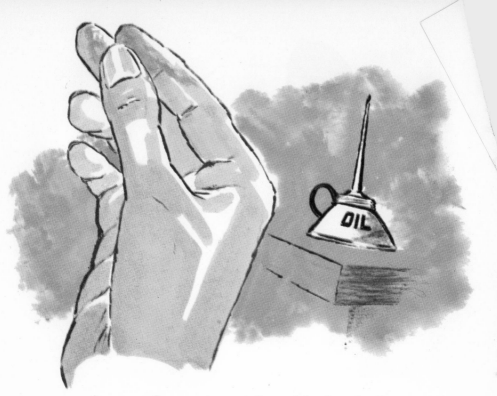

A second way to get less friction is to
use oil.

Rub your thumb and one finger together.
Feel the friction as you rub.

Now put a drop of oil on your finger.
Rub your thumb and finger together again.
It feels slippery, doesn't it?

Your thumb and finger move very easily
and smoothly now.

Rub two pieces of toast together.
You can feel the friction as you rub.

Then spread butter or jam on each piece
of toast. Spread it good and thick.

Now rub the pieces of toast together
again. The butter or jam fills up the
hollows and covers the bumps in the toast.
The pieces of toast rub smoothly against
each other.

You can finish the experiment by eating
the toast.

We use oil and grease on machines to
make them run more smoothly.

Do you have a bicycle or a wagon? If
you do, turn it upside down.

Spin the wheel and see how long it
turns before it comes to a stop.

Put a few drops of oil where the wheel
and axle come together.

Spin the wheel again. See how much
longer the wheel turns now.

The oil makes friction less between
the wheel and axle. It makes the wheel turn
more smoothly and easily.

When we put oil or grease on machines, it makes them last longer.

The parts of the machine will not rub against each other so much. If the parts of a machine rub together very much, they will wear out.

This is why automobiles are taken to the service station to be greased.

This is why we put oil in the machines we use in the home.

We can use other things beside oil and grease to get less friction.

Sometimes drawers stick and will not pull out very easily.

Rubbing the underside of a drawer with soap or a candle will cover the bumps and hollows. The drawer will now move smoothly and easily.

Soap and candle wax also work very well when sliding closet doors are hard to move.

A third way to get less friction is to move things by rolling rather than by sliding or dragging them.

Here is an experiment to show this.

Pull a book across the top of a table. Feel the pull of friction.

Now put many round pencils in a row on the table.

Put the book on the pencils and pull the book again. See how easily it moves now.

The book rolls over the bumps and hollows. It does not slide or drag across them.

Rolling friction is less than sliding friction.

A wheel makes use of rolling friction. The wheel rolls over the bumps and hollows. In this way the wheel does not rub across them so much.

There is less friction with wheels and rollers.

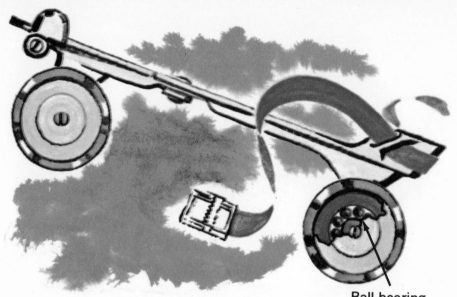

Ball bearing

In some machines there is friction between the wheel and the axle.

To get less friction, small metal balls are put between them. These smooth round metal balls are called ball bearings.

When we use ball bearings, the wheel does not rub against the axle so much. The ball bearings roll between them, and we get less friction.

There are ball bearings in the wheels of roller skates and bicycles.

This is something you can do to show how ball bearings give us less friction by rolling.

Put a book on the table and spin it. It will not spin very well, because of friction between it and the table.

Now put a metal cap from a large glass jar over some marbles.

Put the book on the metal cap and spin it again. The book will spin many times.

The marbles act like ball bearings. They roll between the book and the table.

Friction can be very harmful. It can wear things out.

When two parts of a machine rub against each other for a long time, tiny pieces of metal are rubbed off.

After a while the parts become thinner and weaker. Then they break.

You can show how this happens by rubbing two pieces of sandpaper together. See the bits of sand fall on the table as they are rubbed off.

Friction wears many things out.

Clothes wear out as they rub against the chairs you sit on. Rugs wear out as you walk on them.

The soles of your shoes become thin as you run and jump and skip and play.

Pencils wear out as you rub them against the paper.

Automobile tires wear out as they rub against the road when the wheels turn.

Friction can be harmful in another way.

When two parts of a machine rub together, friction makes them hot.

This heat means work and energy wasted in fighting friction. Sometimes this heat will harm the machine by making the parts melt.

Would you like to get heat from friction?

Rub your hands together hard. See how warm they become.

Rub the eraser of a pencil back and forth many times on the table.

Now put the eraser quickly to your upper lip. Friction makes the eraser warm.

The next time your father saws wood, make this test. Touch the metal of the saw before he begins to saw. Then touch the metal after he stops.

The metal is warm because it rubbed against the wood while cutting it.

Yes, friction can be harmful.

But friction can be very helpful too.

Without friction you could not walk.
With no friction between your shoes and the
ground, your feet would slip and slide.

This happens when there is ice on the
ground. There is very little friction
between your shoes and the smooth ice.

We use friction between the automobile
tires and the ground to help the wheels
start moving.

When we push down on the brake pedal,
friction between the brakes and the wheels
helps us to slow down or stop.

When an automobile is on smooth ice,
there is very little friction. The wheels
just spin around and around.

When this happens, we can put sand on
the ice to give us more friction. Sand makes
the ice rough.

Or we can put chains on the tires. This
helps make the tires rough.

There are many things you could not do
without friction.

You could not turn a door handle to open
the door.

You could not tie the laces on your shoes.
The laces would not hold together.

You could not run or play. You could not
hold a ball or a bat.

You could not color with crayons, write
with a pencil, or use chalk.

Yes, we need friction very much.

What Have We Learned About Friction?

1. When two things rub together, we get friction. This is because the things have bumps and hollows that catch and stick.

2. There is more friction between two rough things than between two smooth things.

3. Heavy things give us more friction than light things. There is much friction between a heavy thing and a rough thing. There is less friction between a heavy thing and a smooth thing.

4. Friction can be harmful. It can wear things out, and it can make things hot.

5. When friction is harmful, we want to get less friction. We can do this by making things smooth. Or we can use oil, grease, soap, and wax. Or we can make things roll instead of slide. This stops things from rubbing against each other so much.

6. Friction is helpful too. Think of the many things we could not do without friction. What are some of the ways to get more friction when we need it?

Words Younger Children May Need Help With

THINGS TO DO IN SCHOOL OR AT HOME

Here are some experiments you can do. Many things look and feel very smooth to us, but they really are not smooth at all. They look smooth to our eyes and feel smooth to our fingers. If you can get a magnifying glass, try looking at many different things through it. Look at your finger tips. See the bumps and hollows they have. Feel the pages of this book. They look smooth, don't they? Now look at them through the magnifying glass. Do they look smooth now? Can you see bumps and hollows? What other things can you find that look different through the magnifying glass?

When two smooth things rub against each other, there is little friction. The next time you wear a new pair of shoes, see how easily you slip and slide when you walk or run across a waxed floor. Rub your fingers over the soles of the new shoes. They are smooth and shiny. There is little friction between the soles and the smooth floor. Now feel the soles of your old shoes. They are rough. They will not slip or slide as easily over the waxed floor.

Can you tell when something needs oil? There are two good ways to find out. First, if it is hard to move, it may need oil. Second, if it squeaks when it moves, it may need oil. Try these two ways on some of the things around you. Does the door hinge squeak? Is the door catch hard to move? Do the wheels of your wagon or roller skates squeak? Is the lawnmower or lawnsweeper hard to move? Your scissors? Your doll carriage? See what happens when you give them some drops of oil. What other things can you find that squeak or are hard to move?

We need friction for many things. Without friction you could not turn the door handle to open the door or you could not unscrew the cap off a glass bottle. Get a glass bottle with a screw cap. Unscrew the cap. It comes off easily, doesn't it? Screw the cap back on tightly. Wet your hands and rub soap all over them. Now try to unscrew the cap again. You cannot do it. Your hands are too slippery now, and there is very little friction between your hands and the screw cap. The same thing will happen when you try to turn the door handle when your hands are soapy.

Without friction you could not light a match. Get a mirror and a piece of sandpaper. Ask your mother, father, or teacher to strike a wood match first on the mirror, then on the paper. The glass mirror is smooth, and there is not enough friction between the mirror and match to make the match hot and catch on fire. But when the match rubs against the rough sandpaper, there is much friction. The match gets hot and catches on fire.

Read about how the Indians made fire by using friction when rubbing two sticks together. Many Boy Scouts know how to do this, too. Perhaps they can show you how they do it.

Friction is both helpful and harmful. There are so many things you could not do if we did not have friction. You could not sit on a chair. You could not hold this book in your hand. You could not hold a knife or fork or spoon in your hand. You could not chew your food. You could not wash your face and hands, brush your teeth, or comb your hair. Make a list of some other things you could not do if we did not have friction.